If It Wasn't for the Earwigs I'd Be Deaf

ALSO BY ROSE AIELLO MORALES

If You Find Zen on the Side of the Road, Don't Tell Buddha
A Life of Small Stories
Requiem for the Girl
A Beautiful Mess
Stages
All These Things I've Done
Visions of You
A Slant Towards the Middle
When the Rapture Comes I'll Be Hiding in the Basement
Prelude to a Coffin Nail
Storm Warning
Naming Names
If I Were You, I Wouldn't Be
Magnolia
Treading Water in the Stream of Consciousness
Watch This Space

If It Wasn't for the Earwigs I'd Be Deaf

poems by
Rose Aiello Morales

Poetic Justice Books
Port St. Lucie, Florida

©2019 Rose Aiello Morales

book design and layout: SpiNDec, Port Saint Lucie, FL
cover design: Kris Haggblom
cover illustration: *Surgical Anatomy, Plate 47*; Joseph Maclise, 1851

All rights reserved.

No part of this book may be used or reproduced in any manner whatsoever without written permission except in the case of brief quotations embodied in critical articles and reviews. Members of educational institutions and organizations wishing to photocopy any of the work for classroom use, or authors, artists and publishers who would like to obtain permission for any material in the work, should contact the publisher.

Published by Poetic Justice Books
Port Saint Lucie, Florida
www.poeticjusticebooks.com

ISBN: 978-1-950433-28-5

FIRST EDITION
10 9 8 7 6 5 4 3 2 1

contents

Where Prayers Go	3
A Woman of Little Consequence	4
Non-Linear	5
Earwigs	6
The Color of Nothing	7
Snow	8
Beach Wails	9
The Sound that Summer Made	10
Light Play	11
A Woman Far from the Sea	12
All Things Being Equal	13
Melancholy Morning	14
An Unclothed Woman	15
Forever Works	16
The State I'm In	17
Ennui	18
Interesting Times	19
Loquacious Laconic	20
Poetic Cryogenics	21
Bleak Horizons	22
In the Absence of	23
Not Enough	24
Thoughts on the Common Man	25
Drink Me Small	26
Burning My Tongue	27
No Legacy	28
Magellan Speaks	29
Ghost Trees	30
Through the Glass	31
Your Shadow at Midday	32

Dust	33
Ledger	34
Like Water	35
No Milk Today	36
Moon Strikes a Bargain	37
She Feels a Sad	38
When Death Calls	39
Re-Imaginings	40
Rethinking Suicide	41
The Lovely Trees	42
Place	43
Echoes	44
Blink	45
Now	46
Apocalypto	47
Sunday Everyday	48
Postcards from Nowhere	49
The Weight	50
Lost Like Novae	51
Those Hours	52

If It Wasn't for the Earwigs
I'd Be Deaf

Where Prayers Go

I am dirt walked through dirt,
clay turned red chalk
through the century drought,
time and calamity,
the age of pestilence,
I am Kafka's nightmare running.
Blink eyes, raise arms,
a diviner for a world of human thirst,
of plants left rotting in the seed,
remuneration comes in drop
drop
drop.
An ark is built too late,
a termite chews the wood,
spits out newborn Christ in seconds
coming through a deluge
that might just save me
if I keep my mouth closed
and stop looking up.

Rose Aiello Morales

A Woman of Little Consequence

Even a whipped beast growls,
the weak judge mediocrity,
transcendence tries the rest.

There the mother lay,
the broken back of circumstance
chastened by the one still standing.

The prisoner escapes, but barely,
harpies appear in her dreams
as women of little consequence.

The very act of their appearance
means everything, and nothing.
The prisoner shrugs in the light of day.

Disdainful of authority and the female mimic,
her closed eyes act subservience,
her unbowed back shows something different.

Non-Linear

Millions of me in my head,
smiling, crying, a treatise on infinity
though time and age do chip away.
Today I learned that time is not a river
but a wash immersion, existing in, outside
of all I know and all I'll come to learn.

A brain trainee, a single atom on my finger,
one infinitesimal moment, focus all around,
a dream is part of life I live in then, now, and forever.

Rose Aiello Morales

Earwigs

I've been waiting for the soul whisperers,
the Holy Spirit crawling in my ear,
singing prophecies and conspiracy theories,
punching numbers, figuring averages.

I've been waiting for these earwigs
to divulge the secrets of the universe,
murmur winning numbers for the lottery,
I keep listening but they never do.

The Color of Nothing

My box of crayons has a leak,
120 has whittled down, one by one
the little nubs have disappeared,
blue sky colored over,
red sun turned to watered pink,
a wash of grey, water colored solvent.
Possessions are a bottle full of gesso,
back to canvas, back to blank
and what is there to do?
I've lost my scarlet to a bloodless coup,
khaki-colored armies trample through,
their brushes morphed to tan Holocaust,
to politicians' semi-truths, to gunwales,
Monday is another word for every day,
now they shoot, shoot, shoot the whole day down.

Rose Aiello Morales

Snow

I see footprints, seconds and they're washed away,
the rain stops for no one.
In flash it passes, then back again,
my feet press against the unknown sodden.
Light mist happens, turns torrent to hard beginnings,
some hint of sun before the molding breaks,
I'm lost in trying, run between drops,
can't find my way home.
A slight more chill and it would snow,
white blankets and a walk way booted
lay a path to where I started,
a guide to where I first went wayward.

Beach Wails

Drawn in the sand a quarter's lunge to the edge
the water flows half way to the blanket,
grains of glass blown into no particular pattern,
popsicles melt in the sticky sun
already sucked dry, this day grows cloudy,
murky, I draw another line, and then another
certain this last will be the one that stays,
indecision raises heads, crabbed along the beach,
claws out, searching for another shell
to hide the inevitable crisis of outgrown arguments,
I pack a blue striped bag as the tide rushes in.

Rose Aiello Morales

The Sound that Summer Made

I thought it was the sound that night made,
Summer's light swept softly 'cross the sky,
in the dark I heard it as it moved,
like violins tuned up for concerts that would never come,
an orchestra bone weary until Autumn
when the players went to hibernation.
I never thought it was a cricket dance,
grasshoppers in a party for the end of day,
rubbing legs in barely held anticipation,
or locusts waiting for the thirteenth year,
the thrill of copulation, for what was sex to do with cabbages,
or babies found in patches? I thought it was the sound that night made,
lullabies to sleep by, tender symphonies left playing on a record player,
waiting for a mother far too tired to ever come and sing the songs,
the stories Sister told until I learned to read the books on bugs,
and sex, of many different things that Mother loathed to talk about.

Light Play

The light of day is brightest when it's hidden,
dreamt by lucid dreamers, long of thoughts,
too full to sleep, the ones with moonscape in their eyes,
tasting, teasing, tasked with memories to spare,
visions given onto streetlamps and the glaze of lower lights.

Memory serves, and they the keepers of the keys,
lovers and regrets, until the morning fails to come,
though they won't enter into dreamless night.
The sight remains with eyes closed, open to the dark
when shades of black reveal the next to come.

Rebirth comes onto the worthy,
Infants swaddled in the womb of time,
flows of water, blood of incarnation,
fragrant dew upon the bow of newborn lips, mouths whimper,
sounding, and a bubble breaks, releasing newfound worlds.

Rose Aiello Morales

A Woman Far from the Sea

When the wind blew just right
our house smelled like ocean,
or the stalls on Fulton Street,
seaweed with a hint of decay,
fish left stranded when the tide rolled out.

I am an albacore left out to dry,
yearning for the tang of salt,
I keep the girl with an umbrella close,
white facets pouring in precipitation,
sand, a letter stoppered in a bottle.

All Things Being Equal

It all adds up. Years and years, months and months,
scant minutes of allotment. Yes, it all adds up to
zero. Leave your beauty or stark ugliness right here,
it all sloughs off. If from the bottle it has come,
back to bottles it will go. The only permanence is
plastic and the gold inlays of teeth. In death we
all will look the same. The Director has one photo,
one size that fits us all. Death erases years, wealth,
sadness, happiness. Door to door among the parlors
there is one face, the one with blonde hair brown
hair black hair white hair no hair. Beards and mus-
tache cover for our sex, but all things being equal,
you can go through any ritual of death, the dead
will tally it as theirs and make their mark, and then
you can go home again and live.

Rose Aiello Morales

Melancholy Morning

Come to me like the absence of light
growing into itself until expulsion,
slow motion rising through clouds
undeveloped, the red glow of a dark room
sad until completion, then still, no happy picture.

Come to me in mourning beige,
crepe myrtle hung by the door,
beautiful in scents wafting,
enveloped in the grief of night's ending,
melancholy morning, I breathe your colors.

An Unclothed Woman

Appearance is the measure of a woman,
so I clothe myself in dowdy,
leave lips chapped and bleeding,
though I obfuscate in many colors.

Appearance is the measure of a woman,
I shed clothes, skin, words,
naked to the world (almost),
but my hair still covers my brain.

Rose Aiello Morales

Forever Works

The look of sadness when it's raining,
flowers yet to come have greedy little tongues,
slurp uncut diamonds from the sodden earth,
ingest bright colors into budding bodies,
leap like sunrise flash into the morn.

Sad will drift away, some tears draw mist into the sky,
grey/blue the subtle hue of clouds' attempts at smiling,
blown away and laughed away, a cow chews cud,
an aftermath of cries and sorrow, cycled back to glow,
and this is how forever works, the come come come
of new days rising.

The State I'm In

*"I don't think they'll ever make me Poet Laureate
of Georgia now" - Me*

This Podunk outpost,
this river to nowhere,
I find Deliverance on its borders
in signs welcoming me from.
Blown tire on the freeway
and I found myself here,
my car was a little bit Country,
I suppose,
when all I wanted was to Rock and Roll.
This non-preponderance of cities,
this absence not much fonder
than snow on the windshield,
floods beneath the wheels,
something I chose
from a one-page catalog,
and here I stay
with anywhere on my mind.

Rose Aiello Morales

Ennui

This chair has an indentation,
buttocks shaped delineation,
unseen by the human I
left sitting endless in this chair.
This chair in the room it sits in,
dust and webs a found fixation
hands that once cleaned do not move
while sitting endless in this chair.
This chair with a window nearby
without eyes it sees the world
the eyes of someone crouched within it
sitting endless in this chair.
Teenage angst and weathered boredom
truth, and lies and indecision
paralyzed, agoraphobic
sitting endless in this chair.
This chair has a bony texture
coffin of the one who lived it
born without but dead within it
decomposing in this chair.

Interesting Times

Fog lays its choke-hold on the day, relentless.
Mist fingers strangle sun,
hold the dawn's light hostage.

A rooster's cries are meaningless,
the hens will not gather
in such inauspicious circumstances.

Its crown deflates, wattles tremble,
the females take no notice.
Day does not commence, a bad omen.

Interesting times are these,
the curse is imminent,
blood roils across the sky.

Sailors drop their canvass,
turn into no wind,
a saying dies upon their lips.

Rose Aiello Morales

Loquacious Laconic

Touch upon people with their handshakes,
secret into society, the jackass kicks and brays
until the waning moon soothes its soul.
We hide when we can, the clouded night obscures
and cats walk, black between the cobblestones,

they keep their notices onto themselves.
Time comes to whispers, vespers cry incognito,
there are loose boards we crawl under,
here in our blessed isolation,
loners talk into these walls,
replace the bricks and mortar.

Poetic Cryogenics

Dali and his clocks, frozen,
not melting on the desert floor,
a memory in shades of tan and beige
distilling painted moisture in the sand.
Cryogenics of the mind,
a dream on ice, the sickness of a nightmare,
thoughts without the pages to distill them,
Thermador a bargain in its way.
On ice, a poem within a poem,
an instance I can travel back to
burning in subzero ways
'til 30 feels like 60, Fahrenheit to Celsius
a comforter to swaddle me when words won't come.

Rose Aiello Morales

Bleak Horizons

Forecasts become more bleak
and the Weathermen return
not knowing which way the wind blows.

Polar opposites patrol the blackened streets,
ice, ice, and baby it's cold outside,
some Global Warming may be all we need.

I'm all for climate change
and someone who understands
what it just might mean for us.

But do not look to institutions,
there is no higher learning there,
simply some magicians sporting redcaps.

I'll be in the basement
mixing up the medicine
for 2020 vision and a bitter cure.

In the Absence of

Air has a flavor,
an unintelligible description,
define clear, and nothing is a taste.

If clarity is truth
and a lie is opaque,
is untruth something you can touch?

Black is the presence of all color,
but halls are black in the absence of sun,
flick a switch and hue are meaningless.

Line your crayons up in darkness,
fill in images with each, together,
until wax obscures the space between lines.

Maybe blackness
is the truth you see
before you see the light.

Rose Aiello Morales

Not Enough

There were 11
black dots
pulled out of the sky,
11 circles of buckshot
and the ping as some hit ground,
grass obscuring
ground opening as it ate squab.
Outrage raised its head,
some others would not raise theirs,
gazed at blackness onto black earth,
feathers not taken by the bluster of wind.
Wings conjured flight
where there was none,
wafting slow until the dirt stopped trajectories,
22 wings drifted from 11 crows,
dead, the perpetrator vindicated,
it was not a murder.

Thoughts on the Common Man

Oh, when the Earth moves,
leaves the best of us behind, if it would just turn around,
reverse its trajectory for one infinitesimal moment,
raise the universal boot off the lowly of the fickle eye
for the reprieve of the common man,
for the Joes, the Jobs, the also rans and honorable mentions
in their drab greys and taped nose glasses,
the Dodge ball targets and whipping boys,
if good guys finished first and the plain girl got her wish,
then and only then would the universe be able to
call itself "fair".

Rose Aiello Morales

Drink Me Small

There's a hard place where the heart goes,
recessed in forgotten lobes
retained from the time we knew no happy.

Now the frontal sings of joy, despair,
water flows, its drops are prescient,
telling us which way to go.

You're a rock shined in places
other times rubbed raw with grief
abandoned in a far-off cave, a shroud.

The stone lies heavy on a chest
of doubt and pain, lifted, you see,
a gem appears in calloused hands

and somewhere in the labyrinth of turns
there is a pinpoint door, a needle of life,
drink me small and you shall find it.

Burning My Tongue

Paper paste to Eucharist,
someone sold me Christ the cookie
but I doubted, so the taste was glue,
yet nothing ever stuck to me,
sloughing off like water from jackasses' backs,
 the priest's eye knowing where I'd been.
I loved the smell, Catholicism in a censer,
smoke blown up my nose,
communion and forgiveness in a wafer,
Heaven in a gilded glass.
Beyond the curtain lay a quandary,
a vision showed my own true self
as bare feet burning on the stairway.

Rose Aiello Morales

No Legacy

You would leave me
violence, dead flowers,
stains upon a couch
you loved more than any of us.
Smelt the links in chains
you would use to bind me,
figurative, but your aim was not,
I still heard the air crackling
as I opened the urn,
hidden in my sister's house,
blew foul air in,
disturbing ashes never meant to stir,
then quick, replaced the top,
so all the bad stays buried like your memory.

Magellan Speaks

Many spots are left,
clear skinned innocence
and the perfect softness of ignorance.

But still, face road maps harbor places
where I tried to lose myself
until paper folded in the right direction.

Lines and lines, a wrinkle speaks
of places I have been,
of trails that fork without an ending.

Now one voice is whispering in my ear,
directional harpy that it is,
and I am only lost in sleeping solitude.

Rose Aiello Morales

Ghost Trees

Once was a meadow
and the grass grew trees,
tall, short, stunted,
some without limbs
until something made them sprout,
lifted them from the ground they fell on,
red in time turned brown, in rings begotten
so that we'd forget, or sanction parkland
where the children play, oblivious.
This soil is iron rich, the saturated ground
saltpeter worth its weight in fool's gold,
earth like powder and the shells haphazard on the ground
are spent, and weeping for the souls well pierced,
planted like the mother trees with life suspended
on their trunks, the very bark alive with squirming,
crawling, growing to become another race,
perhaps now peaceful in this place of dead and living.

Through the Glass

A door stands to everywhere, nowhere,
on the inside dents appear
around the splintered walls
and burnt out feelings
crumbling into rubble
where I stand, I sit, I lie in riddles.

On the outside, bills of lading,
I've seen them come, watched them go,
past due notices of failings
and I close behind them,
stranded in the hall,
calls of vastness fall upon deaf ears.

I have a peephole where the world shows darkly,
circled glass to tell the times
when I have reached a hand, a foot,
struggled, searching for the sun,
cobwebs always pull me back,
bells ring three times, I sleep, I dream.

Rose Aiello Morales

Your Shadow at Midday

You say my poems ramble,
I never find objectives,
the best being short,
straight between lines of departure.

Your tall tales shrink in midday's sun,
a beam directly overhead,
revealing points of reference,
all becoming blind by light.

I love that time of day,
eyes visions of incandescence,
heat upon an upturn,
you become a vanishing point.

Dust

The softest glaze
of rainbow gossamer silk
threads through a light time wind
into bands of forever universe,
eon seconds falling into dream speak
flux and flow, a quill captures ink
before exact moments, anticipation,
kiss breath upon love's echo skin.

Hot, breath of Hell's hounds laughing,
What is that you say?
Way of worlds, way of words,
way of shatter screaming in the night,
a huff of fire singe throat,
two syllables, a syllabus, the ashes of a thought,

Dead sounds falling into vacuum.

Rose Aiello Morales

Ledger

They torture me with weaponry,
shoot barbs upon my ailing flesh,
there, in the undercurrent behind eyes,
my accusers stand within the darkness, flashing.

Judges, execution, my transgressions scrolled before me,
days and sequence numbered, demons squat upon my soul,
a dark mare prancing in the abyss, in the mists of illegitimate
the scales roll out, the night becomes a rocky start, the outcome hazardous.

Tossed, they turn among themselves, slash upon a ledger,
checks and balances, the motives of a wasted life,
and I, round pupil and unconscious eye, see more than shown before,
they roll their dice before the coming of the dawn, snake's eyes are glittering,

A new day comes, and I do not repent.

Like Water

Fragile, these things in the known,
like an amulet against death,
some piece of fluff we keep until we no longer need it,
it floats away when our hands are not vigilant,
perhaps to give another some surcease.

I tried, once, to hold water in my fists,
jealous, a save that never did need saving,
open palms could bring it to my mouth,
closed, it seeped between some little noticed fissures
until nothing much remained but the memory of wet.

Rose Aiello Morales

No Milk Today

Comes dripping from the barren teat,
fountains turned, on/off
like the whims of motherless children
weaned all too soon.

Cream will not rise to the top,
in these times of homogenized syrup
the postman doesn't ring at all
and the milkman died long ago.

It poured today,
broken bottle glass in prism
and the salt of the earth stayed buried,
human kindness is not overflowing,

I think it may never rain again.

Moon Strikes a Bargain

Here, locked as Earth exerts its canny pull
fluidity of souls will bear its tides,
this winter moon is grave, without a tug,
my heartstrings never stirred except by ebb and flow
now unto rivers winding, spring so far away, unraveling.
One fall from rocks and nooks,
a cavern hidden by liquidity parts a curtain of the sea,
some grains of sand's imaginings, phantasms following
a salt drenched ocean, dark stars lose their arms.
Glow uncovered, pocked orb only shows its evening face,
reflections of another's light, and with the bright day down,
dawn breaks a mirror image; will luck hold fast onto its hand?
No, just aces, eights as night relinquishes its woes.

Rose Aiello Morales

She Feels a Sad

Something in the atmosphere that blue cannot erase,
blank against some prisms, hidden raindrops,
please, no songs about a grey sky's actions,
clandestine as some such doings seem.

Emotion runs along a crooked street
where fires are banked against the coming of the sun,
a dog lies panting beneath broken morning's edge
and cats are dreaming of their forays into long extinguished night.

A woman walks along a bright and winding road,
some just picked lemons weeping in her hand,
oblivious of happy child's intrusive fist
which pulls on sorrow's threads and hanging skirts.

When Death Calls

The day of my death has come and gone,
today, today, and every today,
tomorrow it will come again.

It greets me every morning
with gifts and songs
I will not accept; my throat does not warble.

One morning I will wake
onto my anniversary,
this day becomes my stone, my bullet.

But now, at dawn I spring,
bone wary from my bed,
and scream at Death "No! Not Today!".

Rose Aiello Morales

Re-Imaginings

Ground gives up its secrets,
buried, long forgotten,
in the urging of a shovel, spade.

A ring, tarnished
cries a tear for love thrown
from hands, a black crow's mouth.

Months lay frozen under winter snow,
some days, a calendar year,
promise ripped apart into its pieces.

Old clothes, a dump on the edge of town,
a house demolished, dream home turned to ashes
and the slats from cribs, to absent occupants.

To the Earth, to the Earth,
all is reincarnated, back as a feather,
skin and bones, a mind remembers.

Rethinking Suicide

See the marks on her street,
Gothic signs denoting failed crossings,
she wants someone to hit her,
dreams of feeling metal
taut against skin,
the vehicle of her redemption.

Perhaps a chemical solution,
bubbles in the glass
a potion for emotion,
but the glass breaks
only at her bidding,
her mind forgets her mind.

And it kills her,
she feels like she could die
but doesn't want to die right now,
no, not right now
when her sin travels with her,
the sin of so much failure.

Rose Aiello Morales

The Lovely Trees

The trees, beautiful, haunt my dreams,
in silent soft, they bend, they hide
they think I do not see, but oh, I do.
The man is there.
Eyes onto the day, a mirror of my steps, pause,
waiting in peripheral, his breath, his heartbeat
screams within my mind meld, thoughts of monsters.
Trees bark their soliloquies of warning.
A leaf distracts attention to its flow
first left, then right, so buoyant in the wind
I watch its motion, down, down
Forget about the man, he is not there.
He is, his pounce becomes he is,
and I am forced, silent, wondering
why must I fear the man?
The man is here, and I am drowning in the air.
The trees are watching,
wrenching time out of my hands,
I gaze at trees, the lovely trees
I will not walk amongst again.

Place

Perhaps it's written on a small white card
signifying where a being should sit
in the rigid hierarchy of the dinner parties
I never had the chance nor inclination to attend.

I am a butterfly landed on a flower,
a wing flap changes its direction,
with the smallest current blown
my history becomes forever changed.

Trains, planes, and automobiles,
a ship that sails upon the sea,
the sorest feet that traverse mountains,
a simple sign announces, "You are Here."

I am an immigrant from everywhere,
my flag is planted on a distant shore
and I am everyone and everything,
a citizen of Earth, I've crossed a line invisible.

Rose Aiello Morales

Echoes

Summer plays with line-less face,
sun across a field of flowers
nodding heads in sleepy heat.

Last hurrahs arrive in sheaves of wheat,
colored leaves of gold, brown, russet,
showers fall like green flash horizons.

Now skeletons of balding trees
stand without their tresses' glory,
snow soon hides October fire.

Blink

There must have been something in my eye,
a tear perhaps, some mundane irritant,
dust from a cosmic wind,
and you, the infant with the soft, sweet skin,
forgive my reflex, I'll forgive your process,
growing, as we all must, time at light speed,
sunbursts from the universe beginning,
a speck within an all too open eye, I blinked.

Rose Aiello Morales

Now

Right,
now is a peculiar construct,
each type stroke a series of nows.

Infinitesimal,
these instant moments,
lifetimes in a single motion.

Don't roll your eyes
you disturb the inhabitants
of an iris universe.

We live
in eternal Now
each time we blink.

Apocalypto

They said that it would end this year
like before, before, and before,
spinning, then the thing just stops
and we stand still, no centrifugal
keeps us landed, but the gravity
of situations ends, we will not leave.

They've said it other times I'm sure
the year, the month, the day
and we would drink, and laugh
find many ways for people without futures
and fall wasted, not bereft, left strangely calm,
awakened the next morning, still the same.

They said that it would end this year,
in fire, and rain, with floods and pestilence,
but witness every morning the same dawn,
blue sky, the tragic magic of the day,
not today, or tomorrow, nor next month,
though next year, maybe next, perhaps, it ends.

Rose Aiello Morales

Sunday Everyday

Sunday is a feeling of guilt
and no, I won't confess,
whoever you are,
I haven't gone to church forever,
this is my first confession since I don't know when.
Mea culpa, my breast is sorely bruised,
which is a lie, but no, I won't confide.
Father, bless me, for you have sinned
you keep a screen between us to hide transgressions.

Postcards from Nowhere

Between the signposts of flux and reality
there in the void reaching,
books with no words, photos over exposed
a postcard from nowhere develops,
drawn in colors of sand, pinks and tones of beige
sharpened in the aftermath of nuclear tests,
the fallout happens everywhere, and nowhere.

Split second eye close and you've missed it,
Levittown transferred into desert,
here where now dead people crouched
behind glass that never would save them,
their bones meshed into cookie cutter kaleidoscopes,
super-sites and the dry hulks of houses,
walk down the cut-up asphalt and everyone knows
this is nowhere.

Rose Aiello Morales

The Weight

Tell me when you find him on his morning round,
sleep waking at 4 am,
calling people who've gone to bed
to tell them how he's feeling.

I dream these hours, fits of swallowing ground,
a pile beside a gaping hole
I've dug enough to throw me into,
prostrate on his withering bones.

Tell me if he bleeds beneath his thorny crown,
his stations never making him a god,
I know he suffers for his litany of sins,
I carry crosses he no longer can.

Lost Like Novae

To friends who flamed too quickly.

Nuclear, we are,
we burn so hot and bright,
beacons in expanse of darkness.

Stars were never meant to die
but burn out slowly,
shows of sparks, eternity.

Look out at the evening sky
onto the dawn that never comes,
the endless drift of endless night

And there they are,
true beacons of the days
before I knew of dreamless sleep.

A meteoric rise,
 a thoughtful eye will gaze
so ignorant of when they fall.

Angels are consigned to earth,
alight, a feather flames onto the ground
and we are young, too young to realize.

We vow to place them back into the sky,
the night returns them now and now,
so then becomes a memory of novae bursting.

Rose Aiello Morales

Those Hours

Every night I close my eyes,
dying until morn,
entering the realm of death
where antecedents speak to me.

I answer in affirmative,
feel their mists congeal,
authentic in the moment
as I almost feel the pull of Heaven.

Heaven is amorphous, tentative,
I touch it only through a dream
and dreams are all that harbor me
'til daylight lifts a lifeless lid.

A cure for languid morphine,
shot red from hardened veins
as dawn now drags me from the grave,
the living stretch their willowy arms.

If It Wasn't for the Earwigs I'd Be Deaf

about the author

Rose Aiello Morales was born in Queens, NY. She studied at Rutgers University before heading to Miami, Florida to seek her fortune. She has been a waitress, a dancer, a factory worker, sold Avon, was a telemarketer, and a school volunteer before she discovered writing. She is now the author of several books of poetry, short stories, and novels. Her writing is eclectic and she expounds on a wide variety of subjects, some humorous, some political, some serious. She currently lives in Georgia with her husband and three cats.

colophon

If It Wasn't for the Earwigs I'd Be Deaf,
by Rose Aiello Morales,
was set with Trebuchet MS fonts
by SpiNDec, Port Saint Lucie, Florida
The jacket and covers were designed by
Kris Haggblom, Port Saint Lucie, Florida

www.ingramcontent.com/pod-product-compliance
Lightning Source LLC
Chambersburg PA
CBHW030133100526
44591CB00009B/636